A Visit to PUERTO RICO

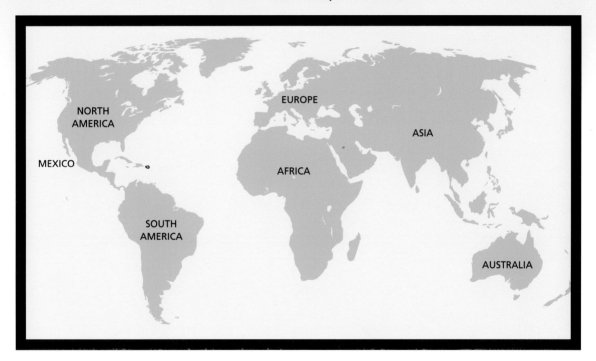

NORTH AMERICA

EUROPE

ASIA

MEXICO

AFRICA

SOUTH AMERICA

AUSTRALIA

Leila Merrell Foster

Heinemann Library
Chicago, Illinois

© 2001 Reed Educational & Professional Publishing
Published by Heinemann Library,
an imprint of Reed Educational & Professional Publishing,
100 N. LaSalle, Suite 1010
Chicago, IL 60602
Customer Service 888-454-2279
Visit our website at www.heinemannlibrary.com

Designed by Sandy Newell
Printed in Hong Kong

05 04 03 02 01
10 9 8 7 6 5 4 3 2 1

Library of Congress Cataloging-in-Publication Data

Foster, Leila Merrell.
    Puerto Rico / Leila Merrell Foster.
        p.cm. – (A visit to)
    Includes bibliographical references and index.
    Summary: An introduction to the land, culture, and people of Puerto Rico.
    ISBN 1-57572-381-6 (library binding)
    1. Puerto Rico—Description and travel—Juvenile literature. [1. Puerto Rico.] I. Title. II. Series.

F1965.3 .F67 2000
972.95—dc21

                                                                00-02953

Acknowledgments
The publishers are grateful to the following for permission to reproduce copyright material:
Corbis/Stephanie Maze, pp. 5, 9, 12, 22, 24; Corbis/Tony Arruza, pp. 13, 14, 18, 25, 26, 27; Corbis/Bob Krist, pp. 6, 15, 28; Corbis/Tom Bean, p. 7; Corbis/Franz-Marc Frei, p. 11; Corbis/Macduff Everton, p. 19; Corbis/James Marshall, p. 29; Tony Stone Images/Mark Lewis, p. 8; Tony Stone Images/Robert Frereck, p. 17; DDB Stock/Jack Messler, p. 20; DDB Stock/Suzanne Murphy-Larronde, p. 21; DDB Stock/Robert Fried, p. 23; Lucid Images/PictureQuest/Mark Downey, p. 10; Donald Deitz/Stock, Boston/PictureQuest, p.16

Cover photograph reproduced with permission of Corbis/Bob Krist.

Every effort has been made to contact copyright holders of any material reproduced in this book. Any omissions will be rectified in subsequent printings if notice is given to the publisher.

Some words are shown in bold, **like this.** You can find out what they mean by looking in the glossary.

Contents

Puerto Rico

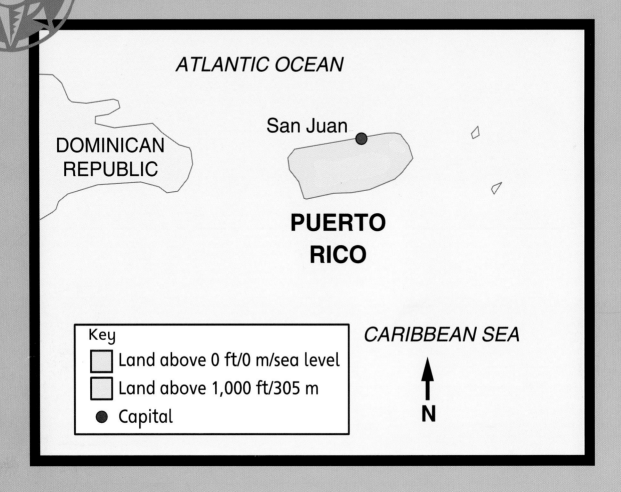

ATLANTIC OCEAN

San Juan

DOMINICAN REPUBLIC

PUERTO RICO

Key
- Land above 0 ft/0 m/sea level
- Land above 1,000 ft/305 m
- ● Capital

CARIBBEAN SEA

N

Puerto Rico is a group of islands in the **Caribbean Sea**. It is miles from the United States **mainland,** but it is still part of the U. S.

The people of Puerto Rico eat, work, go to school, and play just like you do. Life in Puerto Rico is also **unique**.

Land

The main island has rocky hills and some mountains. It has good **ports** for boats. The beaches are sandy.

The weather is warm. Some rain falls almost every day. There is a mountain **rain forest** there. It has waterfalls, animals, and big plants.

Landmarks

The **capital** of Puerto Rico is San Juan.
The best-known landmark is a fort called
El Morro. People from Spain built the fort
hundreds of years ago.

Puerto Rico has one of the largest **radio telescopes** in the world. It is used to study stars and gas clouds. It is in a big hole in the ground.

Homes

Most Puerto Ricans live in cities. In the **capital,** some people live in houses or apartment buildings. There are some old buildings and many new ones, too.

In the country and in the mountains, houses may be small. In the old days, houses were made of wood. They had roofs of **palm** leaves. Today most houses are made of **concrete**.

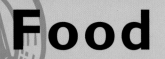

Rice and beans and fish are favorite foods. **Spices** like hot peppers are used to flavor foods. Many Puerto Rican foods first came from Spain and Africa.

Many kinds of fruits grow in Puerto Rico. There are pineapples, bananas, and oranges. People also like coconuts. People can buy them at fruit stands.

Clothes

Puerto Ricans usually dress in warm-weather clothes. Children often wear T-shirts or shirts with short sleeves, and shorts or jeans.

Sometimes people dress up in special
clothes. The boys wear straw hats and
cotton shirts and pants. Girls wear ruffled
blouses and skirts.

Work

In the cities, many Puerto Ricans work in factories. They make clothes, medicines, and computer parts.

In the country, farmers grow **sugarcane**.
Coffee is also an important crop. Many
people also work in fishing. Fishers catch
more lobster than any other kind of fish.

Transportation

Cruise ships stop at San Juan. They bring **tourists** to the islands. Airplanes and ships connect Puerto Rico with other countries.

Puerto Rico has good roads. They stretch
from **coast** to coast on the main island.
People use cars, buses, trucks, and cabs
to get around.

Language

People from Spain **settled** Puerto Rico, so most people speak Spanish. Spanish uses some of the same letters as English.

Puerto Rico is part of the United States, so many people also speak English. Sometimes people speak a mixture of Spanish and English called "Spanglish."

School

Children must go to school from the ages of six to sixteen. The lessons are taught in Spanish. Children also learn English. Many children wear school uniforms.

Many Puerto Ricans go to school even when they grow up. They study at universities and colleges.

Free Time

Baseball is a favorite sport in Puerto Rico. Many Puerto Ricans have been stars of major league teams. Roberto Clemente was a famous Puerto Rican baseball player. He had 3,000 base hits.

Water sports like fishing, **surfing,** and swimming are popular. Many people **scuba dive** to get a close look at fish and sea life.

Celebrations

During some festivals, people dress up in costumes. There are parades, rides, dancing, and singing. Puerto Ricans celebrate the Fourth of July and Presidents' Day, too.

Most people in Puerto Rico are Roman Catholic, so religious holidays are very important. Some holidays celebrate special people called saints.

The Arts

Music and dance in Puerto Rico mix Spanish, Native American, and African beats. There are many **folk dances** that people still dance.

Musicians play drums, **gourds,** and guitars. Some famous musicians got their start by playing on the street.

Fact File

Name The Commonwealth of Puerto Rico is the country's full name.

Capital Puerto Rico's capital is San Juan.

Language The people speak Spanish and English.

Population There are about four million people living in Puerto Rico.

Money The money is called the dollar.

Religion Most Puerto Ricans are Roman Catholic.

Products Sugarcane and coffee are important crops. Chemicals, food, machines, and computers are sent to other countries.

Words You Can Learn

hola (OH-la)	hello
adiós (ah-dee-OS)	goodbye
sí (see)	yes
no (no)	no
gracias (GRAH-see-ahs)	thank you
por favor (pore fah-VOR)	please
uno/una (un-oh, un-ah)	one
dos (dos)	two
tres (trays)	three

Glossary

capital	important city where the government is based
Caribbean Sea	sea south of Florida that is part of the Atlantic Ocean and that is near Central and South America
coast	land at the edge of an ocean
concrete	manufactured stone used to make buildings
cruise ship	big ship that takes people who are on vacation from place to place
folk dance	dance that people in a country have danced for a long time
gourd	large fruit with a hard shell that can be dried to make cups, bowls, or musical instruments
mainland	main part of the United States
palm	tree without branches that has large leaves at the top and that grows well in warm places
port	place where boats can stay
radio telescope	special instrument used to study the stars with radio waves
rain forest	deep woods with tall trees where rain often falls
scuba dive	to swim underwater with air tanks and masks
settled	moved from one country to live in another country
spice	dried, ground-up plant used to flavor foods
sugarcane	kind of tall grass that can be made into sugar
surfing	riding the waves on a special board
tourist	person who visits a place while on vacation
unique	different in a special way

Index

More Books to Read

An older reader can help you with these books.

Kent, Deborah. *Puerto Rico: America the Beautiful.* Chicago: Children's Press, 1992.

Kummer, Patricia K. *Puerto Rico.* Mankato, Minn.: Capstone Press, 1999.

Welsbacher, Anne. *Puerto Rico: The United States.* Minneapolis, Minn.: ABDO Consulting Group, 1998.